Life - A celebration

Ojasvini Chaturvedi

BookLeaf Publishing

India | USA | UK

Presentation by *BookLeaf Publishing*

Web: www.bookleafpub.com

E-mail: info@bookleafpub.com

ISBN: 9789358319910

First edition 2023

DEDICATION

I want to dedicate this to myself, my parents, husband, my son, my family and friends.

ACKNOWLEDGEMENT

I would like to acknowledge all those people whom i have come across in my life. As an observer i would like to appreciate them all.

PREFACE

This book describes different feelings, emotions and how important is to be grateful that we have this life.

As a person i have learnt to appreciate and be grateful of the breaths i have and things i am witnessing in this life. This book has different themes which describes various emotions, time and human's existence.

Questions Unanswered

Typical instances in life, give a roller coaster
ride,
From the day a person is born.
He is found cribbing, struggling all along,
QUESTIONING, WHAT DID I DO SO
WRONG?

Throughout his childhood,
He enjoys without thinking much for tomorrow.
But as the person grows, learns and reflects his
life,
QUESTIONING THE LORD, WHAT DID I DO
SO WRONG?

This ride of life has a lot to offer
Weather you realize or don't bother
Keeping things on the side
Raising the question to Almighty
WHAT DID I DO SO WRONG, THAT I
DIDN'T DESERVE RIGHT?

As the person grows
Life shows different modes
Some of them good, some of them bad

All rated on the perception in one's mind he has
set
If things happen good & nice, he feels happy &
absolutely fine.
If wrong hmmmm…..
The same old question arise lord!! What did I do
so wrong in this life, THAT I DIDN'T GET IT
RIGHT?

Thinking of wrong & right in his life,
He losses hope, his precious time
Not counting his blessings, being grateful
thankful of this life
Questioning the same old question
Oh My Lord!! Where are you in my wrong &
what did I do that I didn't get it right all the way
long??

Survivor's Route

Capability to survive
Can be understood by those who are willing to
thrive.
Some leave this life by losing the fight,
Others watch-by saying
That silver lining will come to our side.
GOOD & BAD moments will come & go!!
The one who is strong enough
Will actually GROW…

Greif, pain, sadness is all part of one's life
Either TODAY or TOMMORROW the SUN
would raise
Turning the board of NO/WRONG/NOT
RIGHT TO THE BRIGHTER SIDE!!

Saying the route, you choose is perfectly right!
HENCE YOU ARE SURVIVOR OF LIFE!!

2 F's OF LIFE (Forget and Forgive)

Forget and forgive, are TWO important
principles which one should follow,
If you accept them, you'll be steady in life.
If you don't then some days you will be made to
realise.
If these principles are inculcated in one's life,
The troubles and tough times would go bye.
So, lets recognise and adapt to these two
important "Fs" in our Life time.

The F's principle works in every aspect of life
If you take it and implement in your life you will
appreciate.
What is the goodness of having and following
These two wonderful Philosophies (Forget &
Forgive) in one's own life.

Easy or Tough

5

It is easy to find faults,
But it is indeed very tough to accept them.
It is easy to see darkness,
But tough to bring hope and light.
It is easy to give advice,
But very tough to implement the same in one's
life.
It is easy to break up,
But tough to stay.
It is easy to lie,
But tough to accept the truth.
It is easy to fall,
But extremely tough to rise.

SO WHEITHER TOUGH OR EASY, IT IS FOR
US TO DECIDE
WHAT TO CHOOSE
EASYWAY OR A TOUGHWAY IN ONE'S
LIFE!!

CHANGE

Change is the only constant thing in life,
Everybody goes through change.
Some change because of the time,
Some with different experiences in lifetime.

Some believe change is nowhere,
Some say change is everywhere.
I also feel things change with time,
A seed turns into a tree, A small boy or girl into
man & women.
This is indeed a major change.

Everything has a tendency to change,
But some see it as nature, age or mere time,
For others it is the change that made their life.

So, friends change is eternal, whether you realise
or not
It will occur, it is occurring.
When you'll lookback you will find some
changes happened,
When you were in different state of mind.

Prayer to God

Ohh God, make me strong,
Give me the power to rise against wrong.
I know life is not easy and we all have a past,
Which moves like a bullock cart, slow and
steady full of jerks.
Where life is also based on one's luck.

Ohh God, save my jerks,
Make this life work.
Help me, help others,
So that I can be together
By together I mean
Make my life "worthwhile"
So that when I can come to you
I have a broad smile and off course with no
regrets in life.

Poetry In Mind

It seems to me years have passed,
Since, I wrote a poetry as fast.
Thoughts flew in my mind,
Making me think have I changed
From a simple human being to
A Philosopher of some kind.

Time has moved on a rapid pace,
Or it is me who has unable to manage time in
first place.
A series of events have taken place
Since, I wrote a poetry at such faster pace.

So many thoughts flew in my mind
Expressing them has become a challenge of
some kind.
But then the philosopher in me said,
Let others figure out what's thoughts flow in
their mind.

Dues

9

Everyone in his life, has some dues to pay,
Some people pay early,
Others have to wait or pay in installment ,
Either too early or late.

These dues are all divided,
It depends on how you find it.
These dues are good or bad,
Which makes the person HAPPY or SAD.

Hence, do as much good as you can in your life,
Otherwise, there is a possibility that's one
wanders hay way
That would be worse than an Exile.

This Shall Pass

This phase too shall pass,
I read this phrase
When time for me was, not running at the right
pace
The time was not passing Through.

My brain seemed to have eaten rust,
My heart had denied to pump,
The body had lost it's current.
Then wind around me flipped those pages,
Which clearly stated that times will turn around,
Sun will rise starting a new phase around.
Just arise, have faith & never give up during any
phase!

Anger - An emotion better to control!

Anger is one such emotional state,
Where your balance of mind is at stake.
The actual control is lost,
Words flow from the mouth without any
thoughts.

One may not realize at that time,
But later when you reflect.
The words spoken shouldn't have been used,
Without applying your mind.

Anger can only do worse,
So better to control and think first.
Look at things around, being the countdown,
I am sure you would be in a better state once the
Anger calm's down.

Thoughts in my Mind

Everybody has mood swings,
There are good & bad times.
People speak and talk when they have some
motive in mind,
But if you express & share your feelings
honestly
Advice comes use your brain before speaking
your mind.
If thoughts are not acceptable or doesn't sound
great to hear,
Then please don't hear them and close your
mind.

So, this makes me think, if I have to express
what's in my mind
Then words should always sound pleasant to the
mankind.
But If I will think of others and express
How will I speak what comes to my mind.
Ohh GOD!
Is there a problem with me?
OR
These honest thoughts coming to my mind?

But if I think and speak all the time
How will I speak what's coming to my mind..

Dreams – Power to Reality

Everyday with a new bright light,
I rise with a new dream in my eyes.
But as the sun becomes bright,
My eyes realize that dreams
Were brighter when there was no light.

My dreams are mere fantasies,
Things I want to do in real life.
But will I do it or not,
That depends on who hard I try in this bright
light.

I believe dreams comes to those, who have trust
to achieve,
The one who tries is the one who gets.
Belief in one's dreams can change how you
perceive things.
Hence, dreams make you realize ,
If you live with them in this real life
You can become what you want with dreams in
your eyes.

Material Wealth

In today's, world where money,
Has become the utmost thing.
Emotions are not worth expressing,
Where promises are always breaking.
Love has no meaning,
Technology has replaced the manual beings.

Children are becoming adults in their teens,
Everything is related to change in surroundings.
Moreover, if nothing works then we blame it on
global warming.
Humans are aware but not willing to take
responsibility.
Nature has started to ask back by sending natural
calamities.
Material wealth has changed everything.
Its time to reflect and change some of our
perspectives.
Money is important but it cannot replace the
living beings.
That's what i believe as a human being.

Hope

Belief is an ever-living thing,
Trust is something worth keeping.
Hope is something which costs nothing,
Family is that where one should be investing,
Human beings are the ones, which possess all
these things.

So come on, lets sing & be merry,
Let's keep hope alive and make oneself win in
this life.
People who dream,
Are the ones who achieve.
So, my friends keep those hopes high, I am sure
it is worth a little try.

Gesture Of Giving

Giving is one gesture in life,
Which everybody must cultivate.
Laughing & making fun of others,
Is easier and convenient
But to give, is a gesture
Not possessed by everyone.

The gesture of giving can be learnt from mother
nature,
Which stands as a mere spectator.
But the day you think of ''Me or I''
There comes the pride
The whole process which you might have
inculcated
Turns aside & becomes a question?
Were you actually having the gesture to give or
it is the ego which had to subside?

Change OF Time

The change of time,
Is one thing which no one can understand.
The only thing one can do is flow,
Flowing with the change, Is true practicality,
An adaptability which one can befriend.

Time has wings, it has been said,
But how many of us actually accept.
Everybody thinks we are the boss
Hence, we would never suffer a loss.
Thus, there comes the time,
When everything is left behind,
The people you love and care, are the ones who
would not be there,
Nor will the time let us all be alive.

So, my friends always flow with the tide,
Otherwise, you will be lost
Better learn to be real
Otherwise, you will feel
HOW?
DEATH is so near and so real.

She- To the women power

She was in a wait for sunshine,
She thought she would surely find
The rise in her life,
The time passed by.
One fine day she realized
That there was no need to wait for sunshine,
It's just her thoughts stopping her to find
What potential she holds even without the
sunshine.

She spread her wings,
She laughed out loud.
She found the way out,
She became the ultimate sunshine
The real power she showed in herself was
divine.

She never stopped,
She never looked back.
She never escaped,
Nor she ever held herself back.
She became the ultimate sunshine
Which she was finding outside all this time.

People Around

Looking at the people around,
Hearing them say the world is round.
Living a life on their own,
Thinking about themselves as grown.

Thinking big, growing large,
Imagining themselves as class apart.
Counting on their material wealth,
The lumpsum bank balance which they have
kept.

A house of bricks build,
But no family to live.
Wanting to live on their own terms,
Leaving their parents at the old age home.
Giving an excuse,
You don't match our pace
Sending them to an unwanted exile, when they
are almost on their LAST STAGE!!

Saying them you don't match the pace,
You always interfere in our ways,
Ask these people where was the PACE,
When they were not aware about the RACE.

It was these parents who introduced them about
Pace,
And what pace would be the best to win this
RACE.

So, my friends do as much good as you can,
So, that tomorrow you are at a GAINER'S END
And history is not repeated
As it is said
And your life is free from any regrets!

Love - An emotion to express

This is a passage for people not in love,
Who think we fall in love.
But love will never let you fall
As there will always be someone
To guide you and be with you near or far.

Love is not blind,
It is like a treasure one of its kind
It comes to those who are lucky to find
Treasure which we all can keep and still we need
not bind
It's an emotion for a lifetime,
A feeling to express & share
Otherwise, you will be left behind

Optimism

Optimism is something,
From which everybody can gain.
Positive people make other people find Hope,
Those who believe are the ones who achieve.

Optimism is a strength
Which can help you overcome all the lacking's
of life.
Life can sometimes be harsh,
But always remember this phase shall pass.
Just focus on your goals
Look after your health.

Now it's up to you how you take it?
Either be unhappy or stick to negativity?
OR
Be happy and stay optimistic.

Incredible India- Thanks to my country

Himalayas on the top,
Oceans down below.
The Dessert on one side,
In the eastern side diverse herbs grow.
The 4 directions North, South, East, West,
Marks the diversity present on every edge.
How do I describe this place
Where everything is so special & great
As various authors, poets & scholars state.

I don't have much words to say, about my
country
But as the tourism ministry has rightly portrayed
"Incredible India", truly great
I too believe in this statement
The Tagline is indeed appropriate
I would like to thank the people and my country,
For being so immensely great.